Voices of Change

Sister Evetha Kilamba

Voices of Change by Sister Evetha Kilamba
Published by Gena Publishing

This book or parts thereof may not be reproduced in any form, stored in a retrieval system or transmitted in any form by any means, electronic, mechanical, photocopy, recording or otherwise without prior written permission of the publisher, except as provided by United States of America copyright law.

Copyright 2006 by Sister Evetha Kilamba
All rights reserved

ISBN 0-9755101-1-8

Dedication

This story is dedicated to my late mother, Pelajia, who taught me so much and inspired me to desire changes. The traditional values she taught me gave me the courage to write this story. This story is also dedicated to my sister, Elizabeth Mmea, who has been a source for me, and too my dearest friend, Bihawa. My mother, my sister Elizabeth, and Bihawa are now gone, but their inspirations will live forever.

I further dedicate this story to my sisters Aloisia, Christina, Helena, Katarina, Cornelia, and Theresia who have shown me great love and support through their letters. Their thoughts, ideas, and suggestions about our family motivate me to think about others. My father and my brothers are included in this family circle.

Most importantly this book is dedicated to all women, especially those whose basic human rights are denied by their societies.

May the voices calling for affirmative change be heard for the benefit of all members of the human society.

Acknowledgments

It would be impossible to adequately thank all of the people who have contributed to the writing of this story. *Voices of Change* would not have been possible if I had tried to do it alone. Many people helped me in different ways. I thank Sister Fokas Mjema, for being available at all times and giving me the courage to keep on writing. Her friendship and great support were a wonderful source of encouragement. I am grateful to each one of my teachers in the English and Women's Studies Departments at Nazareth College for giving me moral, social, and academic support while doing my undergraduate studies at Nazareth College. I would also like to give my sincere thanks to all the teachers in the Masters in Education programs at Nazareth College. The fruit of their teaching is my eagerness to be of true service to everyone in my society.

Gina Battisti, a wonderful friend in Chili, offered much encouragement in the writing of this wonderful story. I thank her for helping me get this story published. I also thank Gordon Walsh for helping by illustrating my story so that people will better understand what I say in it. I further wish to express my gratitude to Susan Tackett for editing and proofreading my story. My very special thanks go to Corrado Zollo, whose effort brought this story into existence. Thank you Corrado for assembling this story.

I offer very special thanks to the Sisters of St. Joseph of Rochester who provided accommodations for Sister Fokas and me while we were studying in the USA. It was under the roof of the Sisters of St. Joseph that I wrote *Voices of Change*. Because of their support, I will take home many resources which will be useful to the people of Tanzania, Africa, and the whole world at large. Finally, I would like to thank my family, friends, teachers, and the sisters of my religious congregation who have made this work possible in many different ways.

Contents

Introduction	7
Chapter One	9
Chapter Two	13
Chapter Three	17
Chapter Four	21
Chapter Five	23
Chapter Six	27
Chapter Seven	29
Chapter Eight	31
Chapter Nine	35
Chapter Ten	41
Chapter Eleven	45
Chapter Twelve	51
Chapter Thirteen	57
Chapter Fourteen	65

Introduction

Traditions can be so deeply embedded in some societies as to override current realities to an extreme degree. As I look at my people, I see the richness of the land and the goodness and intelligence of its people. *Voices of Change* is a story of some of the traditional values that have affected people in that society. Although the story focuses on the Washambaa people of North-East Tanzania, it certainly would apply to other societies in the world where human rights, whether based on gender or other criteria, are being denied using tradition as an excuse. Someone said that dictatorial mandates, from whatever source, always abuse the oppressed and never the oppressors.

In this story, I point out how women are denied education or are victims of traditional inheritance customs. The purpose of this story is to describe some such traditions, and thus to offer women the choice to say NO to oppressive traditions and choose life over death. Nyungu, by tradition, is the power of death which only Washambaa women are believed to possess. This tradition has been the source of great sadness in many of our families. Yet, to this day, women believe that it cannot be revealed to anyone unmarried. It is for this very reason that in this story Nemphao never learns any more about what killed Anapela.

Men and Women of all societies, anywhere, are urged to foster life-giving customs and beliefs. Voices from the mountain were given great importance. These ancestors' voices were used to forbid girls to attend schools and thus become victims of forced marriages. *Voices of*

Change, challenges people to listen to the voices of the real people they can see and hear rather than to voices of unknown, arcane, ancestors. Further, if the ancestors were able to give reasons for natural events, why would they not be able to predict social diseases such as AIDS and the like? *Voices of Change* is a wake-up call for change. It is honorable to respect and obey our ancestors. However, respect and obedience are not to be mistaken for blind obedience to traditional ways that deny basic human rights to anyone.

As you read *Voices of Change*, explore in your mind human rights abuses and consider ways to uncover and change discriminative customs. Consider, also, how you can support the unprotected. I firmly believe that if we listen to ourselves and those around us, we can discern "voices" that can lead us to make a positive difference. You, reading this story, are started on the way to improve the ills of bias and discrimination.

Evetha Kilamba

Chapter One

The Voices of the Ancestors

     Mount Kungu ja Yamba is the source of life for the Washambaa people. This mountain is the source of all the water used by the Washambaa in the Mtindii village. Kungu ja Yamba lets the villagers know when one of them does something. Warnings from the mountains are supposed to be heeded and resulting commands obeyed. Immediate action is supposed to be taken to stop whatever might have made the ancestors angry. The ancestors call the people at the bottom of the mountain to make sure none of the rituals are broken.

Chonge was a very bright girl from Mtindii. After taking the standard seven national exams, she was selected to go to Makuyuni Secondary School. Her mother took her to school and she returned home the next day. The following night, very heavy rains fell on the land. The rain caused floods and many people lost their crops and other belongings. The villagers believed Kungu Ja Yamba had trembled and that the ancestors were speaking from the mountain.

On the following day, the advisors of the tribe gathered to interpret the signs and voices from the mountain. Sheshui, the ablest interpreter of the mountain, was asked to interpret the voices. He had great power and influence in the tribe. He had three wives and twenty-four children. He would be relied on to interpret the voices and would relate to the Busara men the words from the ancestors.

In this instance, he said:
"Why has Chonge gone? We are sad because Chonge is disobeying.
Bring her back. She is our daughter. She is Shemhilu's wife. She is the mother. She broke the rules. We want her back. Where is the kitchen? Where is Mbereko? Chonge is killing us. Busara, you are killing us. You are all killing us. You are chasing us away. We are crying. We want to stay. Bring Chonge back. We want to stay."

The Busara began discussing Seshui's message immediately driven by his strong emotion and convincing words.

The men realized they had saddened the ancestors greatly by sending Chonge to attend a secondary school, out of town. They now knew the reason for the ancestors' tears, and they immediately decided to send Chonge's father to Makuyuni's Secondary School to bring her back to the village. Chonge's mother cried and tried in vain to stop her husband. Her words and tears were ignored. The villagers would only acknowledge the tears of the ancestors from Kungu Ja Yamba.

Chonge was brought back to Mtindii the same day and thus her schooling stopped.

Chapter Two

A Husband for Chonge

On the following day, the Busara met to discuss what to do to relieve the situation that had made the ancestors sad. Sapela, a newly elected member of the Busara group, suggested that Chonge be severely punished by taking her to Kungu Ja Yamba and sacrificing her to the ancestors. Shewili, the youngest of the group, thought that was not a good idea. Shekuavu suggested that Chonge be married to one of her sons without bride price for Chonge's family. The wise man, Sacesi, thought it would be good if Chonge went around the village telling others what she had done so that other girls would avoid committing the same mistake. All six men gave their ideas about how Chonge should be punished. Finally, Mangoshwe, the eldest and the wisest in the Busara group, spoke: "You have all spoken, and your voices have been heard. Now I speak. I think it would be good to find a man for Chonge from within the village. Her husband should be one of us, a Washamba. He should have more than one wife so that Chonge could, then, be taught what women are supposed to do in our tribe."

Mangoshwe's idea was well received; the Busara group all responded "Kweli" which means: "We agree." He, then, adjourned the meeting by saying, "Wazee twende! Twende!" which means: "Old and wise men, let us all go!" They all replied, "Let us go."

The next day, the men from the Busara group went all around the village seeking a husband for Chonge. Sheshe's son, who was attending school, was seen as the perfect match for Chonge; however, he refused because he was still in school. The Busara group did not reveal the boy's refusal. He had spoken, and his words were heeded. So the men continued their search for a husband for Chonge: next, they found a man who already had two wives, was a lot older than Chonge, and agreed to marry her.

Chonge's father was asked to tell his daughter of their decision and to prepare her to get married in two weeks. Chonge received the message with great sadness. Her mother also spoke out, but nobody paid attention to their words. In the village, their voices were not as important as the voices from Kungu Ja Yamba. Chonge's father said the decision was already made. Chonge's mother shed tears as if her daughter were going to die: however, in the end, she reminded her daughter that she was a woman. She told her it was necessary to obey the voices of the ancestors because if they were ignored, the Mtindii village might be destroyed. Chonge listened and started the material preparations for her wedding but, in her heart, it did not make sense. She wanted to continue with her schooling even though she knew it was impossible.

Three days later, Sapela told Sheshui the Busara group would bring the bride price for Chonge. The bridal price would only be one cow and three sheep, instead of the usual four cows and three goats, because Chonge had disobeyed the tribal ritual by going to school thus causing the ancestors to become sad. Sheep are not usually used for the bride exchange in this tribe. They are, instead, paid for girls who have broken the rituals of the tribe. It is insulting for the parents to get a sheep as a bride price. Chonge's mother would not receive any bride price because she supported her daughter's wish to go to school.

Sheshui heard the bad news and asked his wives to prepare a meal for the men who were going to bring the bride price. The next day, the bride price was brought and Chonge was taken by her husband.

The Busara group was satisfied of how they had atoned for the evil done to the ancestors. They thought a very fair action had been taken against a girl who had broken the rules.

Chapter Three

Passing on the Story

Chonge's story was passed on to all future generations of the Shambaa people. Young girls grew up aware that disobedience to the ancestors could bring ruin to the village. All the girls made sure that they didn't offend the ancestors again as Chonge had done. The girls in the village of Mtindii did not dare to ask about Chonge. Their duty was to make sure not to shame their mothers.

Nemphao, one of the girls, collected firewood from the Kigango forest for cooking and for heating the house. Nemphao's father was very happy that his daughter worked so hard. He had no doubt Nemphao was going to please the ancestors and that she was going to be blessed with a fine husband who would pay a good price for her.

Many of the boys in the village loved Nemphao and desired to marry her. Whenever she would go by the bar where the boys were drinking, they would all come out and you could hear them say: "She will be my wife. She will be mine. She will be the mother of my children." Nemphao never stopped to talk to any of the boys; she was also aware of Chonge's fate, and, thus, knew she could not go to school like the other girls from other parts of the country she had heard about.

One night, after her sister Muiwa's wedding, Nemphao decided to ask her mother about Chonge's story. Her mother told her never to repeat that story because other young girls of her age might hear it. Nemphao's curiosity, however, made her mother realize there was a need for her daughter to know the truth. Anammea, Nemphao's mother, emphasized to her daughter not to repeat the story to anybody because it was sacred. Subsequently, she began telling her Chonge's story, as follows:

"Chonge was a girl who made our village's ancestors very sad. Unlike other village girls, Chonge did well in school, like the boys, and she passed the standard seven exams. With a joyful heart, her mother took her to the Secondary School in Makuyuni. This was not something for women;" (Anammea emphasized). "Boys were allowed; but it was forbidden to girls. Our ancestors established it so and it is forbidden to change it."

Nemphao listened very carefully and wanted to know even more. She asked her mother how they knew that the ancestors were sad.

So she asked: "Who said the ancestors were sad for Chonge's education?" "The ancestors themselves told the villagers", Anammea responded. "Our ancestors are dead; hence they are gone. How could they speak to the village?" continued Nemphao. "Nemphao, do you see Kungu Ja Yamba?" said Anammea solemnly. "Yes, mother," Nemphao answered.

Anammea continued, "Our ancestors speak to us from Kungu Ja Yamba. They live there with voices heard only by men. If a woman would report hearing voices from Kungu Ja Yamba, it would be bad luck because it is believed it may not be true since it is reported by a woman."

Although Nemphao's mother spoke for a long time, she did not seem to answer her daughter's questions. Nemphao could not hear enough of Chonge's story. She wanted to hear more. She wanted to know more about the ancestors that people believed were living in Kungu Ja Yamba. Therefore, the dialogue between the mother and daughter continued.

Nemphao insisted, "Mother, I want to know more about the ancestors who live in Kungu Ja Yamba and how they indicated to the people that Chonge should leave the Makuyuni Secondary School and return to the village."

Anammea complied and answered, "It was the night after Chonge's mother returned from taking her daughter to Makuyuni for her secondary education. That night, there was a heavy rainstorm with severe flooding. Many people lost their belongings, although no life was lost. The next morning, a group of wise men, the Busara, met to discuss the natural disaster. One of the wise men said he heard the ancestors in Kungu Ja Yamba speak. They all, therefore, called for the best interpreter of the voices of the ancestors from Kungu Ja Yamba."

Nemphao listened very carefully as her mother told the story.

Anammea continued, "The interpreter said the ancestors were angry because Chonge had gone to secondary school.

The interpreter warned that if Chonge did not return, the Mtindii village would be destroyed. The Busara ordered Chonge's father to go to Makuyuni to bring back his daughter. Chonge was brought home the same day, and was married to a man that already had three wives."

"So, mother, the Busara believed voices from that rock?" Nemphao asked with sadness.

"Yes," Anammea replied, "because those are the people who protect us and have the power to destroy the village if we disobey."

"Why are their voices heard only by men?" Nemphao inquired.

"Because our ancestors are all men, their voices should only be heard by men," Anammea explained.

"But aren't there any women ancestors?" Nemphao wondered.

"Yes there are, but they don't talk to us," Anammea answered sadly.

"Why not?" asked Nemphao.

Anammea even more sorrowfully responded, "Because no one will listen to the women ancestors. They protect and talk to us, but they don't speak to us as loud as the male ancestors."

The story saddened Nemphao deeply. Bravely, her mother told her not to be sad because she could speak to the women they would listen to her. This motivated Nemphao to tell all the young girls and boys about Chonge's story.

Chapter Four

Wanting to Climb a Tree

Every morning, Nemphao went to a nearby stream to fetch water for her mother. The stream was small but very beautiful. The girls from Mtindii liked to get water from the stream every morning to help their mothers and would collect avocados that would drop, during the previous night, from a tree along the path to the stream. Although the tree was on Anapela's plot, the villagers understood that it belonged to the whole village. Anapela never stopped the girls from getting the avocados, but she would remind them not to climb the tree. Some of the best and ripe avocados were very far up in the tree, and the girls would wish they could climb the tree and pick them. Old Anapela would look at the girls without saying anything. She knew they would not try to climb the tree.

The desire for the avocados from the tree urged Nemphao to ask questions. She thought it was good for the girls of her age to know why they should not try to climb the tree. Old, wise Anapela anticipated Nemphao questioning; she could sense it; therefore, she began telling why girls are not supposed to try to climb trees. Anapela explained that if the girls got up in the tree, boys passing by might look up and see the girls' underwear, and that was not good.

As Anapela was talking, a boy, whose name no one knew, passed by. Anapela asked him to climb the tree and get avocados for the girls. The boy could not understand why Nemphao and her friends would not do that themselves. They all looked healthy, energetic, and able to climb; yet, they chose to sit and wait for the avocados. The boy obliged old Anapela and picked the fruit without questions. When they offered him some, he refused and left respectfully.

As the boy turned the corner, he looked back to the girls and said: "You know you can do it." At that the girls ran towards him and asked him his name; but he did not stop and they never found out who he was.

Nemphao and her friends returned to the stream where Anapela was sitting on a stone. They thought it would be good to know more from her about girls not allowed to climb trees. Anapela expected more questioning; so she started talking about the power of the Busara group. She told them how they went to Makuyuni to bring Chonge back from the school. She also told the girls about the power of the ancestors who lived at Kungu ja Yamba. The old woman continued on with ten stories or more, but did not finish any of them. Finally, she said to the girls that she understood why modern girls try to do things that they are not supposed to do.

"Climbing a tree is for boys, not girls," said Anapela in a very authoritative tone. She looked and sounded very wise; however, she never really answered any questions. Her explanations and short accounts on behavior for girls did not fulfill their curiosity. Finally, the girls started putting their containers on their heads and headed back to her own household. Anapela was left alone sitting on the stone, looking down. She was in deep thought about what she had seen, heard, and been asked by the girls from her village.

Chapter Five

Our Girls Should Never Climb a Tree

The shadows cast by plants and trees had moved only a short distance when Anasesi, another woman, passed by the stone near the avocado tree where Anapela was sitting. She saw Anapela and greeted her. Old Anapela did not respond in her usual way; however, seeing that Anasesi wanted to know what was troubling her, she began relating what had happened earlier. She explained how the girls from the village had come to fetch water from the stream and had wanted to climb the avocado tree. At that, Anasesi was very shocked. She re-assured Anapela that the older and wiser women would have a meeting to tell their daughters about what to ask and what not to ask.

So Anasesi and Anapela left and went house by house to talk to the women who were home. There was no-one at Anammea's house, the mother of the inquisitive Nemphao, except Mwashi who had moved to the village three weeks earlier after getting married to Handi. Mwashi wanted to know if she could take a message and give it to her mother-in-law when she returned. Anasesi did not want to discuss the subject with a new member of the village; therefore she told Mwashi that she would return later. When Nemphao came back from school, her new sister-in-law told her that some women were looking for her mother but that they did not want to share the topic with her. Mwashi explained that one of them was the old woman who lived nearby and owned the avocado tree. Mwashi did not know the second woman, but she said she remembered seeing her when the women were preparing to send Mwashi's mother the bride price. She mentioned that these women were going to return later that evening because they seemed to have a very sensitive and important matter to discuss with their mother.

After hearing her sister-in-law, Nemphao went to get water for cooking supper. After she returned, she went to the storage area near the kitchen and took down some dried cassava and started preparing it for the evening meal. At that time, every girl in the village was pounding cassava or soaked corn. The sound of the pounding tools was heard throughout the entire village. Soaked corn was the favorite meal in Nemphao's household; however, that evening it would be cassava since they had eaten soaked corn the night before. You could tell how many girls were in the village by the sound of the pounding.

While the girls were pounding dried cassava or soaked corn, the boys made fire in the "sigii" and warmed themselves. Nemphao's brother, Chambi, brought birds to the boys for roasting. Other boys brought corn and some ripe bananas to roast on the "sigii." The boys always waited outside to be called in to eat.

As it was getting darker, Anammea and her husband Shekuavu arrived from the farm. Anammea had firewood, yams, spinach, and ripe corn in a basket that she carried on her head. On her back she carried a baby. She looked very tired. Her husband was following behind her carrying nothing but a bush knife. As the children greeted their parents, Shekuavu reminded Anammea to hurry up and cook the cassava meal because he wanted to go to bed. Anammea answered her husband with great respect, and went into the kitchen quickly to make sure the meal was cooked properly. She always reminded her daughters that a good wife is one who cooks tasty meals for her husband. It is always best to make sure the water is boiling before putting the flour in. If the flour is put in without having properly boiled the water, the meal would stick to the fingers and it would be very hard to eat. All the daughters were very obedient and good listeners. They prepared the meal correctly. Watching his daughters cook, Shekuavu had no doubt that each of his daughters would get a fine husband.

Chapter Six

The Escort

As the family was sitting waiting for the meal, Chambi came in with Anasesi. Everyone was very surprised to see Anasesi in their house at that time. It was very dark and not safe for women to walk outdoors alone. Nemphao's father always reminded his daughters to be sure to be escorted by a boy when walking outside. That is why Anasesi came with nine-year-old Chambi. It was safer to walk with a nine-year-old boy than for two women to be unescorted at night. Washambaa spirits are very obedient to men no matter what their age. Most of the time, they don't listen or provide protection to women who are alone. The presence of Chambi reinforced the message Anasesi was bringing to Anammea.

Anammea welcomed Anasesi and invited her to stay for the cassava meal. Anasesi said she could not stay because she had left the water almost boiling at home. She had three daughters but no son. Her husband was not home. He was drinking in a nearby local bar called shimoni. After they had exchanged greetings, Anasesi asked Anammea if they could go out for a while. Chambi was asked to go with them, but kept his distance so as not hear their conversation. They found a good spot near the house and sat down. No one could hear what Anasesi and Anammea were talking about. After an hour, Anammea returned to the house and said she could not believe that Chonge was in her house. Nemphao, who was putting aside dried fish and yam leaves for her father and Chambi, listened carefully to her mother, and pretended not to pay any attention, although she was all ears.

As Anammea went on, her husband asked her which of his daughters was Chonge. She did not want to tell her husband because she knew he would not let her have supper. Instead, she told Nemphao to serve dried fish and yam leaves to Shekuavu and his son Chambi. All the girls ate in the kitchen with their mother while the sons ate in the bedroom with their father. It is also a sign of respect for Washambaa daughters-in-law to please their fathers-in-law. During the meal, Shekuavu's daughter-in-law brought in the bedroom a dish of cooked bananas. The men ate the cassava meal and the cooked bananas they received from the daughter-in-law. When they finished the stew made of dried fish, Chambi called Nemphao to bring some more. Mammbago took the container and served the stew. It was a very good meal, but it was consumed with some apprehension because the girls were concerned about what Anasesi had reported to Anammea. The girls suspected something wrong, but no one said anything. Meanwhile, it got completely dark. All the chickens, cows, goats, and sheep were inside. The girls went to bed not knowing what had gone wrong for any of them on that day. Shekuavu told all his daughters before going to bed that he would not keep any Chonge in his house. They all turned in wondering what had made their father so angry. But Nemphao knew.

Chapter Seven

Nemphao Makes Her Father Sad

The next morning, Shekuavu woke up very upset. He told his wife to let all his daughters know he would be sad to learn that they had tried to climb a tree. He could not talk to his daughters because it was against the tradition for men to speak to their daughters. He was afraid that if his daughters tried to climb a tree, they would never get married. His goal was to have them all marry so that he could have as many cows as possible. After all, he had given cows to his son Handi's in-laws when he got married. He knew that all the cows would be paid back when his daughters got married. Shekuavu got worried hearing that his daughters were trying to do things that were supposed to be done only by men. Night and day he appealed to his ancestors to help make his daughters stop doing things that are supposed to be done only by men.

One day he saw Nemphao climbing a tree. He called out with a very anxious voice. "Nemphao! Nemphao! What are you doing? Stop climbing that tree! Call your younger brother Chambi to climb for you. Come down and never try to do such a thing again!"

Nemphao came down with her eyes wide open. She did not call her brother to climb the tree for her. She just sat down for almost ten minutes doing nothing. Her father did not move. He looked at his daughter. Inside his mind, he was contemplating how the Shambaa tradition was being ruined by tradition-breakers including his own daughters. Fifteen minutes later, Shekuavu called his son to help her.

Nine-year-old Chambi climbed the tree for his sister and picked some peaches. Nemphao showed her brother which fruit were ripe. Chambi was too young to know. Shekuavu was happy to see his daughter obey him and allow her younger brother to climb the tree for her.

When they finished picking the peaches, they all went back into the house and started eating the fruit. Chambi was curious to know why his sister was not allowed to climb the tree. He remembered being told by his father that he was not like his sisters. He was reminded several times that, like his three older brothers, he was responsible for keeping the clan of the Wakilindi people going, but he had never been told that he was the only one allowed to climb trees. After all, Chambi had seen his sisters climb the tree several times. As he started questioning his sister, Shekuavu stopped him and told him to be obedient. He separated him from his sister and told him that part of his role as a man was to climb trees, take care of the animals, protect his sisters, and get involved in things that men are supposed to do. His father reminded him he was to roast corn while his sisters were cooking. Chambi obeyed his father and helped his sisters. He never let his sisters climb the tree. He always wanted his sisters to be happy.

Chapter Eight

The Death of Sheshe

"Come here! Come here! Come here!" Nemphao called out to her sister Mammbago who was playing by the road. A group of men were walking and singing, and appeared to be carrying someone dead. Nemphao did not want her sister Mammbago to see a dead body, because she was impressionable and would find it difficult to sleep at night. When the men passed by their house, Nemphao's father joined the crowd to help carry the corpse to his home. As the cortege moved on, Nemphao wondered how the man had died and was very anxious to find out from her mother when she got back from the farm. While still following with her eyes the men, she saw a group of women coming from the same direction the men had came from. They were all crying; however, one woman was crying particularly hard. Nemphao wondered why no woman participated in carrying the dead man.

Later that night, both Shekuavu and Anammea, her parents, came home very tired. Anammea asked her to expedite the cooking because she and other women from Mtindii were going to sleep at the house of the dead man. The girls asked their mothers what had happened to the man. Anammea told her daughters that a tree had fallen on him while he was harvesting sugar cane used for a local drink. All the girls felt sad because they heard the man was from the Busara group. They wondered why the ancestors did not warn about the falling tree that would kill him. What if the tree had fallen on a woman and killed her? They all knew that women are not allowed to climb trees. Further, they wondered, it was strange that men could be killed by fallen trees, since they had the full knowledge and authority to climb them. How could this have happened?

As Anammea was completing the preparation of the meal, one of her daughters asked her whether the ancestors had predicted the death of this man named Sheshe. Anammea did not want to talk about it. She told her daughter, instead, to hurry up and bring banana leaves so that she could carry some cornmeal with her to the mourning home. Every woman in the Washambaa had to take food to the house of a dead person. So Anammea directed Chambi to go with Muiwa outside to cut a banana tree leaf. Muiwa and any of the other daughters could go with Nemphao, as long as they did not go outside alone. Chambi and Muiwa got the banana leaf for Anammea and she tied the meal up in it to take it to the mourners.

As Anammea's home was on the way to the dead man's home, three other women, on their way there, stopped by to wait for her. They all entered the house and started talking about how the death of the man had brought sadness to his household. He would not collect the bride price of his three daughters. They also added his wife would be inherited by another man. They all hoped he would not be abusive with her and use all her farmland to feed only his own family. Mwashi, very recently married, asked if the woman could avoid being given as an inheritance to another man. The women said she could not because she would need a man to protect her.

"A man to protect her?" interrupted Nemphao.
"Oh, God! This is really a shame," said Anammea.

"Nemphao, why are you interrupting older women?" Anapela asked. "No wonder this girl wanted to climb an avocado tree that day."

All the women told Nemphao to be careful about what she said because it might prevent her from getting married. Muiwa also told her sister not to interrupt older women again. Nemphao obeyed and kept quiet.

All the women packed their food and went to Kivumbi to mourn the death of Sheshe. During the night, all the men stayed outside to slaughter and roast a cow. The fire felt warm and all the passer-bys were generously invited. Early in the morning, the men dug a grave to bury Sheshe. It was very sad to hear Sheshe's widow and daughters cry. The three sons were quiet and tried to comfort their mother, but she was crying so hard that no one could stop her. She knew that the death of her husband would open a new page in her life. All the men and women stayed to mourn for three days. On the fourth day, Sheshe's widow, her children, and all their belongings would be given as an inheritance to another man.

Chapter Nine

The Inheritance Ceremony

Decisions about inheritances in the Washambaa tribe are made by men only, because women are not allowed to be involved.

The procedure was for the widow to sit down in front of the council of the wise men of the tribe and make her choice from the group picked by the wise men for her.

Early in the morning, Sheshe's widow met with the wise men from the tribe. They indicated the men from which she was to choose her next husband. The potential husbands included several men that had been close to

Sheshe and even her own son. However, the men said to her that her son should not be her first choice because he did not have the power of a grown-up. She would have to wait until full authority was given to him when he had a connection with the Busara. Sheshe's widow was very sad about this because she had considered her son to be one of her first choices. After reviewing all possibilities, the widow washed her body to purify herself before choosing her new husband.

After that Sheshe's widow talked about the situation with her daughters. All her daughters suggested that their younger brother inherit their mother, because they knew that, if their mother was going to be turned over as an inheritance to another man, she would lose the rights to the house, the farm, the animals, and the bride price that would be paid when they got married. They also knew that when their mother became an inheritance, she would be as a wife to the man, even though it was not necessary for her to love him. Further, after the choice was made, the woman had to become obedient to the inheritor. Sheshe's children preferred their younger brother for their mother because they knew that he was not going to have a marital relationship with her. However, she had to make a vow of obedience to him.

The drum of the inheritance ceremony was played by an expert. Everybody knew this was a most important moment for Sheshe's household. The men sat in a circle. For the first time since Sheshe's death they called by her name, "Nengeo, come out." Nengeo walked alone very slowly and sat in the center of the circle. Her daughters were not allowed to be present, so they sat in the house anxiously waiting the outcome of the ceremony.

Shekuavu spoke with authority: "Nengeo! Nengeo! Nengeo! You are a widow. Today we have to provide for you a husband to protect you, your children, your farms, your animals, and to make sure no man steals the bride pride price which will be paid for your daughters." He continued: "The man that will inherit you is one of the men sitting in this circle. It is acceptable for you to pick your own son. In any case, the ancestors in Kungu ja Yamba will indicate to us whether they approve the choice."

At the inheritance ceremony, a woman was not allowed to ask any questions. She was to offer some water to the man she thought would take care of her, her children, and the wealth of the family.

While Shekuavu was speaking, Nengeo was wondering what would happen to her and her children. In her life, there had been several such ceremonies. The results had not been happy for the widows and their children. In those few minutes, Nengeo made a daring decision never made before by the preceding widows. As she started going around the circle of men with the pot of water, all the men had their eyes wide open expecting to be the one who would be asked to wash his hands in it.

All men, as Nengeo started moving around with the water, were thinking: "It would be really good to have this woman as my wife. Look at the number of daughters Sheshe left. He has so many cows, goats, and sugar cane fields. Sheshe has left a lot of goods and that really helps define a man as a man. I hope to be asked to wash my hands in that pot of water."

"Look, she is so beautiful! I hope she will be mine," Sabeni spoke out loud.

Nengeo's son, was sitting, looking, and listening to the wishes of these men to get his mother. He was sad because his father had gone, and now he was feeling even worse because his mother was in this situation. Unlike all other men sitting around the circle, Nengeo's son wished the inheritance custom had never existed among the Washambaa. As a man, he had to show respect and wait for his time to be asked to wash or not wash his hands.

Nengeo had gone around most of the circle, but she had not yet asked anyone to wash his hands. Most of the men began worrying because they all knew that as the widow would go past them without asking, there chance for the inheritance would vanish. It was customary that the widow could never back-track around the circle and ask a man to wash his hands after passing him the first time.

The men started murmuring, "Oh! look! What does she want to do? Oh! Busara, speak out! Oh Kungu Ja Yamba, where are you? Oh, Sheshe our friend! What is she doing? This has never happened before." The men began complaining when Nengeo stopped in front of her son Kibua and asked him to wash his hands to signify her acceptance of being given as an inheritance to him. Kibua did not know about inheritances, but he had been told that when a woman asked him to wash his hands during the inheritance ceremony, it was a sign that she wanted him to receive her as an inheritance. Having such little knowledge helped the young man not to think too much. He just washed his hands. Kibua was nine years old. The only son left in the Sheshe household received as an inheritance his mother, his sisters, and all his father's belongings.

When the men finished the inheritance process, they all walked away. Sabeni uttered: "Woman, you have picked a nine-year-old, your son to receive you as an inheritance.

We all take this as an insult. We know you will need us. It will be hard for us to obey a nine-year-old. You should have picked me. We all have the desire to respect Sheshe's memory, but you spoiled it. We will see."

"Stop complaining about respecting this boy. He is a man. He is not a woman. He can do all that men can do. So let us respect him and respect his mother's choice." Sasesi said to Sabeni.

Kibua knew nothing about what it meant to acquire all the authority. However, he understood that his mother had good intentions for picking him out over all the grownups. He and his mother returned to the house. All the daughters were sitting quietly waiting to know who their new father was.

Nengeo was supposed to go to greet all her daughters for the first time with her new husband. The husband would then give all the daughters water to drink, and the daughters would kneel until they finished drinking it. Then the man would shave the heads of his new children to mix the locks of each one's hair with his. This signified to the family that he were like their biological father.

When Nengeo opened the door, Kibua went in and said to his sisters; "I am your new father."

They said all together, "Eka Maa" which means, "You are kidding." Joyfully, the girls embraced their brother and they vowed to respect him just like their own father. Nengeo cooked a meal for her husband. Although Kibua did not understand what was going on, they all enjoyed this new beginning in their lives.

Chapter Ten

Choosing a Wife

A few months later, many boys began visiting the late Sheshe's household. The boys knew Sheshe had been a hard worker and that he had died accidentally, working at his farm. Those events brought respect to his family. All the boys wanted to become Nengeo's sons-in-law. The boys would argue about who would marry Nengeo's daughters. In the evening at the roasting corn and birds that they had killed during the day, the boys would discuss what they had to do to get ready for marriage. They knew the girl had to wear a special dress for the wedding.

They said, "We saw how Mahemba got married to the man from Gonja. She wore a white dress and she had something on her head. She looked wonderful!"

"I would love to marry a woman dressed like that when I get married. I would not want to get married by going into some people's house and take away the daughter," said Duku.

"Oh! But that is how we usually get married. We abduct a girl from her home, and then some men from the Busara clan go to her father the next day and tell him that one of their sons has taken his daughter," explained Kibua.

The boys asked if amongst them any belonged to the Busara clan so that they could hear more about this tradition.

"Yes, I am from the Busara clan," Duku responded. "My grandfather Sanimbo used to attend the meetings. I heard my grandfather was present when the Busara group decided to get Chonge back from Makuyuni where she was to attending the secondary school. I heard Chonge disobeyed the ancestors and a very heavy rain poured over the land. The rain almost destroyed the whole village. As soon as she returned from school, the rain stopped and the whole village was peaceful."

Kibua asked, "Do you mean it was okay for the Busara to stop Chonge from going to school?"

"Yes! Yes! Yes!" responded Duku with excitement. "However, we should not continue stopping girls from going to school. The Busara control is becoming a thing of the past, and we are part of the future. We should all be determined to build a better future for both girls and boys. I think, if we do that, we will be better fathers and the girls will be better mothers."

"Look," he continued, "when Sheshe died, his wife was to be given as an inheritance to a man who was supposed to be from the Busara group. These men wanted to inherit that woman so that they could get the wealth Nengeo and her husband had accumulated together. We should all make the village a better place and more suitable for all; therefore, as we prepare for the marriage of Sheshe's daughter Kiungu, her mother has the right to receive the entire bride price. Also, we should remind ouselves that Kibua is a man just like those who claim to hear the voices from Kungu Ja Yamba. So, he should be respected as such and be allowed to manage the bride price within his family. Listen Duku, we do not have to follow what came from Kungu Ja Yamba. Those people are from olden times and are on their way out; we are staying here to change our way of life."

Duku persisted, "We always say, 'When an old person dies, the library burns.' It is better for us to let "the library" burn and forget all the decisions derived from the rumblings of the mountain rather than continue with old customs that cause sufferings for some of us. We should all concentrate on getting a bride and preparing for the wedding instead of thinking about the use of the bride price. Our fathers have obeyed so many unknown things from the past. In our time, we should concentrate on what we know and make sense to us, not to the unknown. We want to keep our traditions going in our own way. The girls of our village work very hard. We can see them going to Kigango to fetch firewood. Look! just now, some of them are carrying heavy loads of firewood which none of us have touched. What's wrong with us? What are we doing here? Let us go and start working in the same way. The village needs to be peaceful, full of hard-working men and beautiful women. Then, we will all have beautiful children."

"What are we doing here?" Duku kept on, "We need to move. Oh! Kibua, do you remember the day Anapela asked you to climb the avocado tree for those girls?"

"Oh yes. I remember," responded Kibua. "Why are you bringing it up? We just said we have to go to work instead of sitting here and discussing the girls. It was hilarious that Anapela would not let the girls climb the tree. Oh! We need to forget all about that old woman. Now, she is very sick. Someone said she broke nyungu. As you know, nyungu is very dangerous. I heard it can kill entire villages."

Chapter Eleven

The Death of Anapela

The Washambaa women had a tradition unique to the tribe. This tradition does not exist in any other tribe. When Anapela got sick, she was not taken to the dispensary run by the nuns. In fact, there was a lot of talk around the village about what Sapela, from the Busara group, did to her that might have made her sick. The ancestors in Kungu Ja Yamba did not say anything related to this sickness. Normally, they only speak when the Busara men have something to say. Anapela's sickness was discussed a lot among the girls and boys of Mtindii. When they went to help each other on their farms, they would sing a song aimed at probing the meaning of Anapela's sickness. In doing this, they related it to the story of Chonge so that the older folks would not understand what they were singing about. The boys and girls sang as follows:

Mtindii, Mtindii, Mtindii, Mtindii.
Kuna mtamu; eh kuna mtamu,
Kuna mtamu; eh kuna mtamu. Mwe ichi kaya
Sen Chonge! Sen Chonge
Mia kuna mtamu, Sen Chonge
Wangwe n Nyungu! Nyungu M Mbwai
Sen Chonge, Sen Chonge, Sen Chonge, Sen, Sen,
Sen. Chonge

This song can be translated as:
Mtindii, Mtindii, Mtindii, Mtindii.
There is someone who is sick
There is sickness in this village
But it is not Chonge.

It's a sickness
They say is nyungu
Is not Chonge. It is not Chonge. It is not Chonge, no, no, not Chonge.

The melody and beat of the song was such that the work on the farm went really fast. The girls and boys could not stop tilling the land while singing. Unless something drastic would happen, they would not even stop to stretch whenever they sang.

At one point, Duku asked for attention by saying: " Listen! Listen! I hear something."

"What do you hear?" asked Kibua.

"I hear someone crying." Oh God!" Nemphao answered. "Someone must have died. It must be true. There are many cries from the village. We'd better stop working and head home to find out who died; probably, Anapela. My mother spent last night at her house because she was very sick. I did not see her before coming to the farm this morning, she must have slept there. Look, a lot of people are going toward Anapela's home sobbing. Some are coming from Yamba. Maybe they are her granddaughters Mfumbwa and Kiao. We'd better hurry home to see what is happening. Nemphao, we are sorry we cannot finish our work at the farm today. We will finish it after the burial and the three weeks of mourning. Don't worry. Everyone will understand that. We'd better go home and see what happened."

All the girls and boys left the farm quietly. The girls did not carry anything with them because they were all going to Anapela's house. Nemphao hid her hoe behind the rock where the family kept its hoes. She could not leave the farm with the hoe because her house was very close to

Anapela's house. As they left quietly, they started asking each other what could have happened to her that made her so sick. They all remembered how Anapela had stopped the girls and boys from climbing the tree. Then they talked about what sickness could take her in just two days and that, if it had been caused by a mosquito or a snake bite, it should be made known to the whole village. The nuns who ran the dispensary should have treated her because they always cure malaria and snake bites. Anapela had a snake bite stone in her house. She should have used it to extract the poison. They all asked many questions, but there was no real understanding of the cause for Anapela's death.

As they approached the home, the women's sobbing persisted. The men had already begun to gather outside the house. They were preparing firewood. The men would spend the night at Anapela's home. Early in the morning, they would dig the grave where Anapela would be laid to rest. When the girls and boys from Nemphao's farm arrived at the mourning house, they wanted to know what had happened to Anapela. The girls entered the house and viewed the body. The Washambaa believe that Anapela could still hear something at this first house, so they all whispered good-bye as they viewed Anapela's body.

Soon after viewing the body, Nemphao was called by her mother to go home to prepare a cassava meal for the family. Her mother told her not to pound any additional flour because what they had at home would be enough. Anammea also told Nemphao that it would not be good for the mourners to hear that pounding, since Anapela's house was as close by.

"I will come home when I find someone to sit near Anapela's body," said Anammea.

Nemphao left the house very quietly. When she reached home, she prepared sardines and yam leaves. She got onions, tomatoes, and carrots for cooking with the sardines from the garden behind the house. Her father liked the sardines mixed with Ngogwe, but she could not find any in the garden. She decided to cook yam leaves, instead. She also knew that the tomatoes and onions would make the sardines taste good. In the garden, Nemphao was thinking about what had happened to Anapela.

Two women passed by, and Nemphao heard them saying, "Sapela must have done something really bad to her. Anapela is not a woman who would break the nyungu. She is not a person who would give up her life. She loved her children and her grandchildren. She always wanted to do what she could to make them happy."

Nemphao was bending over in the garden pretending that she did not hear anything. The two women went on talking about how bad it was to break the nyungu.

One woman said, "If Anapela has put the nyungu near the river, the whole village might be affected. More than one person could die."

"No! No! No!" said the other woman. "She would never do that to the village. She must have decided to die by herself. Also, if the men feel sure that the nyungu was broken, they would not let her spend two days in the grave."

When Nemphao heard that, she got really scared. She wondered what they were going to do with her after she was buried. She thought it was not good to punish someone who was already dead. What were they going to do with her?

"This was not fair," she said to herself. When the two women realized that Nemphao might have heard them, they left quietly. Nemphao also went back to her house and started to prepare the meal for the whole family.

After all the hens were in, Anammea came into the house. She asked Nemphao to hurry up because her husband Shebughe would come home soon. She also knew that her husband was going to stay at the mourning house overnight so that he could help to dig the grave the next day. She did not want him to be hungry as he spent the night at Anapela's home. Anammea was very pleased that her daughter Nemphao had prepared the meal. She realized how her daughter had grown. The smoke in the house was clearing. Everybody started the house chores and were asking what to do next. The young children did not want to stay outside late, especially when someone had died. They were afraid they might see the deceased or that they would see her by the avocado tree in the morning; so, Mammbago and her brother Chambi went into the house and waited for the meal there.

While preparing the meal, Nemphao asked her mother what had happened to Anapela. She did not want to tell her mother what she had heard from the two women who passed by the garden when she was picking tomatoes and onions. She wanted to hear it from her mother and she wanted to ask about what would happen to Anapela after three days. She also wondered if the ancestors in Kungu Ja Yamba had said anything related to Anapela's death. She did not dare ask her mother. She knew her mother would talk about it. Nemphao was sure her mother would not hide anything from her because she was growing into a woman. But, Anammea knew that her daughter had been questioned by many women for saying and doing things that are supposed to be said and done by men only. She respected her daughter and she was ready to listen.

Chapter Twelve

Discovering Nyungu

"Mother! Mother! Mother!" called Nemphao. "I am sorry we did not finish our work on the farm today. When we were in the middle of tilling the fields, we heard someone crying and decided to stop. I remember you told us that if someone died in the village, we should stop tilling the land. So we stopped, but we decided we would go back to finish our turn after the three weeks of mourning.

"There is no problem," responded Anammea. "It is always a blessing to stop tilling the land when somebody dies. You know when someone dies, he or she goes into the soil, and the crops are planted in the soil. We don't do any planting while there is a death. It would be a curse. If the person who has died gets angry, the farm may not produce any crops for the same number of years as the age of the person who has died. If Anapela was fifty years old, the farm may not have a good yield for fifty years. So you made a good decision to stop tilling the land when you heard the cries."

"Thank you, mother," responded Nemphao.

A few minutes later, Nemphao spoke out in a very polite and respectful tone, "Mother, what did Anapela die of? She did not vomit or get a snake bite. She never went to the dispensary. We never got to visit her or send any water in the evening. We never did anything to help her to get better. How could she die so quickly? When I was picking tomatoes and onions in the garden, I heard two women saying something that I did not understand."

"What did they say?" Anammea asked.
"They said it was nyungu," answered Namphao.
"What does that mean?"
"How did you hear about that?" Anamea wanted to know.
"It was while I was picking onions and tomatoes," Nemphao explained.
"You are not supposed to hear anything about nyungu," her mother said.
"Why not?" Nemphao asked.

Anammea spoke solemnly, "Nyungu is supposed to be heard and talked about by women who are married. When you get married, you will understand it. Now I cannot tell you what it is. It is really a poison to talk about nyungu. Let us not talk about it."

Anammea then tried to change the subject by saying. "Hurry up and prepare the cassava meal. Your father is going to be here soon. We don't want him to spend the night hungry."

"I am cooking, but I just want to know what this nyungu is," Nemphao insisted.

Anammea answered, "I already told you only married women are supposed to know about it."

"Can it hurt other people beside the one who did it?" Nemphao asked,

"Yes, it can destroy the whole village," Anammea replied.

Nemphao could not help questioning further, "Is it similar to the story of Chonge going to Makuyuni which made the ancestors in Kungu Ja Yamba talk?"

Anammea anxiously said, "No, it is not like that. This is very dangerous. We should not talk about it because you are not married. When you get married you will know what nyungu is. But if you don't get married you will never know about it."

"So I have to get married to know all about nyungu?" Nemphao kept on.

Anammea explained, "Yes, but if you do not get married, you will not need to know about it. You are not going to have a man around you who can make you think about dying. You will just be alone. But remember, not getting married is a shame which you should avoid. You should always think about getting married."

"Sapela must have done or said something which made Anapela angry and so she decided to kill herself," Nemphao said.

Anammea reluctantly replied, "Oh, yes! That is how men are. Hurry up, Nemphao. Stop talking about nyungu. You are not married. You are not supposed to know about it!"

Nemphao responded in a soft voice, "Mother, I am sad because I see I will never know what nyungu is and how it is done."

"You will know about it. You get married and you will learn about it from other women, not from me. The food is ready," said Anammea firmly.

When Anammea's husband got home, the conversation between the mother and daughter stopped. Anammea refused to tell her daughter what nyungu was and how it was supposed to be done. Nemphao was really sad, but she figured the best way to find out about nyungu was to go to the burial the next day.

She said to herself, "I will go to Anapela's funeral tomorrow. If I see the group of women, I will join them and listen to what they are saying. I am sure that by doing so I will understand that nyungu is what they are going to do with Anapela because of what she did."

She hurried up and put out the cassava meal, sardines, and yam leaves. Shekuavu enjoyed the meal thoroughly. The food was so delicious that he could not believe that Nemphao was the one who had cooked the meal. Anammea reminded Shekuavu to wait for her so they could go together to spend the night near the body of the late Anapela. Soon they finished eating. They told Muiwa to make sure all the children got to bed early. No unmarried girl was allowed to be part of the mourning at night. So, Muiwa and her young sisters and brothers went to bed when their parents left the house. It was a very frightening night for them, but Shekuavu told Muiwa that that they should not be worried because they had a man in the house. That man was the seven-year-old Chambi who was not able to fight off anybody. They all fell asleep thinking about Anapela's death without saying anything. Nemphao feared that Anapela was going to come back to life and she did not want to see her again.

Chapter Thirteen

The Burial of Anapela

Next morning, Sapela, Anapela's husband, picked the plot where she would be laid to rest. It was a place very close to her house. They had to dig the grave in such a way that Anapela's head would be facing away from her home. As she was laid to rest, she would be assigned the duty of protecting her family and her whole village. Her body was gone, but her spirit remained. Unlike Sheshe who had become one of the ancestors, Anapela would not. She couldn't speak to the village, to her family, to friends, or to her children. Her voice would not be heard as she would not be moved to Kungu Ja Yamba. Only special women would have the power to be moved to Kungu Ja Yamba. While the men were digging the grave, the women were sitting inside the house by the bed where Anapela was lying. Some women who were close to Anapela cried, while those who were not close to her sang songs about God.

Anammea and Anasesi had a special role during the death of a Shambaa woman. They had to dig the first grave called kizana. This grave is where they must place all the water used to wash the body of Anapela. In it, they must put the soap, the wash cloth, and the last clothes worn by Anapela before she died. It must be dug under the bed where Anapela was lying. No one could be allowed inside the room except Anammea, Anasesi and the other two women who would help them to move the body away and then back again. This grave is not supposed to be covered until the men finished digging the grave outside and were ready to bury Anapela. When they finished washing

Anapela's body, they dressed her in a one-piece gown that covered her from her head to toe. The gown was sewn quickly, and after that time no one was allowed to view the body. Subsequently, the men returned to the house and told the women that the grave was ready. The women took Anapela's body from the bed and placed it in the coffin and closed the top. The rest of the work was done by men.

Sepela said words of sorrow to his wife; he stood by the coffin and said: "My dear Anapela, I met you when you were a little girl. The day you where born your father gave you to my father. I was not opposed to this, and I loved you right away. I know Busara speaks louder than fathers and mothers. I know we raised our children and our grandchildren together. I know we shared the bride price when our daughters got married. I thank you for being a good wife. You never questioned me. You always said yes to me. You made me feel like a man. Now, you are going before me." Sobbing and shaking, Sapela continued talking to his wife, "Please Anapela, don't come back. Don't be an ancestor. You know you are not supposed to do that as you told me so many times. Remain a woman. Protect our granddaughters from becoming Chonge. May they remain women. None of them should ever try to be like a boy. I will stay here and take care of our farms, animals, visitors, children and grandchildren, our in-laws, and all the people who will join the family you helped me to build." Finally, he cried out, "Uwi! Uwi! Uwi! If I did anything which made you angry, forgive me. I have no power over your body. I know how the men will treat you because of the way you died. It makes me very sad to have an empty grave. Wherever you will be placed, stay well. I will always treat your grave as if you were still there. We talked about nyungu when we were young. When we got older, we never talked about it. We thought it was for middle aged women. Now, my wife, you are going. Go well. I respect

Busara and the voices speaking to us. I will come to you, but I will never be able to lie by your side." He finished by saying; "You are going. You are finished. Your life is nothing. My life is something. I hope my daughters will never die the same death as their mother."

After Sapela finished talking, the men surrounded the coffin and carried it to the grave. They had to bury the body even though they would come to remove it later that night. The children and grandchildren of Anapela cried. They knew their mother was going to be buried, but the grown-ups knew that at night, the village men would come to open the grave and remove her body from the village. The younger ones did not know anything about this, and they would never know unless they got married and bore children. When the men finished covering the grave, Anammea and Anasesi ran back to the house to cover the first grave called kizana. It could not remain open because the outside grave was already covered.

People waited to hear the announcement about the distribution of Anapela's clothes, cooking utensils, and her hoe as an inheritance. Sapela also had to decide about whether or not he wanted his daughters to be given as an inheritance. On the same day, Sapela made the decision that he did not want his children to be given to anyone as an inheritance. He said he wanted to take care of his house and that he would decide whether to re-marry or not.

He called the men from the Busara clan and said, "I don't want to give my daughters to anyone as an inheritance. I will think about whether or not I want to re-marry. Today, I am not going to make any other decisions. I will speak with the village men now, but I may not share my decision with anybody because I am a man." The Busara men respected him and left the place.

Sabeni, who was making the announcements, called the crowd and said, "We are all set to come back Monday. The women will cook cornmeal and the men will slaughter a cow. We will all eat together. This is not the time for the men and women of the village to think about who might receive an inheritance. We will leave that to the zumbe of this household. We should now leave; if someone wants to stay, there will be tea and porridge later. Men and women from near and far, let us leave and allow this household the time to learn to be without their mother, wife, and grandmother."

All the men left. Anammea and Anasesi could not leave the house until Monday. Since they had dug the first grave, they had to stay until the grave hardened. They knew that, during the night the men were going to open the outside grave and take Anapela's body to Kigango and leave it there. They would not leave Anapela's body in the village because it might cause the death of other villagers as she died because of nyungu. Anammea and Anasesi had to stay there to make sure no one from the house went out at night. The two wise women did not want Anapela's children and grandchildren to know how Anapela's body was going to be treated. They all stayed in the house quietly. At midnight, the men removed the body and carried it to the forest. As they left it there, they were not allowed to turn and look back. If one of the men did so, the sprit of nyungu that was with Anapela's body might follow them. If this were to happen, another woman might die because of nyungu. The men didn't want this to ever happen again, and so they left the body without looking back.

Three days after Anapela's death, the people got together to clean up the house. They ate meat and cornmeal. Anapela's daughters and grandchildren shaved their heads. A lock of their hair was taken by a man from the Busara clan. Anammea took the lock from Anapela's oldest daughter. Together, a Busara man and Anammea went and buried the locks of hair at the grave-side.

Mfumbwa asked, "What are they doing with the locks of our hair?"

"They have to bury them so that we can be united with our mother," Kiao responded.

"But grandmother is dead," Mfumbwa kept on.

"No, she is not dead," Kiao explained. "She just went to another place."

"Is she going to be an ancestor so that we can hear her talking in that rocky place?" Mfumbwa asked.

"Mfumbwa!" exclaimed Kiao, "Don't you dare call it a rocky place. It is a place that must be respected."

"Okay!" Mfumbwa agreed. "So we will be united with our grandmother, eh!"

Anammea shook her head and remarked, "These days, children are so disrespectful. I, too, have a daughter who always questions everything. I hope one day she will stop. This will hinder her from getting married."

Kiao looked at her and said, "I am really worried about the way Mfumbwa talks about going to school."

Anammea nodded, "Nemphao also wants to go to secondary school. She even told me she wants to be a nun."

"A nun?" Asked Kiao with surprise in his voice.

"Yes," responded Anammea, "She wants to be a nun. She said she will never get married."

"Oh! That is dangerous," Kiao said. "When she dies, she will be forgotten."

Anammea sighed and said, "That is true, but what can I do?"

Kiao reflected out loud, "Look! We are sitting here together now because we are Anapela's children."

"Yes," agreed Anammea, "but I believe my daughter can have children in the church."

"So you support her idea of becoming a nun?" asked Kiao.

"Yes, I do," Anammea answered, "because she will say whatever she wants to anybody. I have eight daughters and four sons. It will not be a loss if one of them does not get married. Her name will be kept by her sisters' and her brothers' children."

"I would never allow my daughter to be a nun," Kiao strongly affirmed. "That life has all the elements of visitors from another part of the world. Look, even the nuns in the dispensary are all visitors."

"But they all help us." objected Anammea. "When we get sick, they give us medicine and we get better. They also teach us how to take care of our children."

"But they don't know about nyungu," Kiao stubbornly insisted. "That is why they will never keep us from doing it."

"They don't have to know aboutnyungu," Anammea interjected. "I also don't want my daughters to know about it."

"That's right," agreed Kiao. "This nyungu is satanic. I wonder why the ancestors never said anything about it. See, now I have to raise my children without their grandmother."

Anammea cautioned, "Let us not talk about this any longer because the girls have their ears wide open trying to find out about nyungu."

"I will never teach anybody what nyungu is," Kiao affirmed, "It is like the presence of a devil in our community."

Anammea's face brightened as she said, "That is why I am happy Nemphao is going to be nun. Out of my eight daughters, I am sure, then, that one of them will never know what this devil is."

As Anammea and Kiao were talking, Shebughe interrupted the conversation and he called out her name three times.

"Here I am!" Anammea answered.

Shebughe reminded her to make sure she went home because someone had to bring water for the goats. Anammea told him that she had told Chambi to take care of the goats and Shebughe was glad to hear that. Anammea told Kiao that she and her husband needed to go home and to let her go into the house from which Anapela was now missing. Kiao reminded her to make sure she came back to sleep with them at night. She knew that the next twenty-one days would be very hard and that she had to teach her children to cope and stop calling out to their grandmother.

"Okay!" Anammea agreed. "I will be back at night. I will sleep here for the whole twenty-one days. There is no problem at my house. Muiwa is there, and she will take care of the young ones."

Kiao thanked her, and Anammea took her basket from her hand and put her hands behind her back. She looked toward Anapela's grave and said, "Anapela, don't get angry. I am coming back at night. Help me to take care of their children and grandchildren. I will be staying here the whole twenty-one days." Anammea told Kiao she was leaving, and he said good-bye.

After the death of Anapela, her husband did not want her children to be given as an inheritance. Sapela wanted to pick a wife of his own choice. He did not want the men from the tribe to make arrangements for him. He did not want to see women sitting in the circle as he moved around with the bowl of water to make one of the women wash her hands in it. None of the women who were in the position of being given as an inheritance to Sapela wanted to marry him. All the women in the village knew that something wrong caused Anapela's death. They knew that she might have been trying to reason with Sapela while she was still alive, but he did not want to listen. They all knew that when their daughters got married, the pride price was supposed to be shared with Anapela, but she was like an unheard voice in her own household. Since no one wanted to be given as an inheritance to Sapela, everyone wished he would marry a woman from another village. The women who did not know him would think he was a good man. But even when they listened to the last words he said to Anapela, while she lay dead, it was clear to them that he was not a good husband. That is why the Mtindii women thought that Sapela might never get married. All the women left the house. After twenty-one days, Kiao, her children, and her grandchildren left the home, too. Sapela was left alone and he was very unhappy. He tried to find a woman to marry, but none of the women wanted to marry him. He died alone a few weeks following the death of his wife.

Chapter Fourteen

Bihawa's Death and Nemphao's Decision

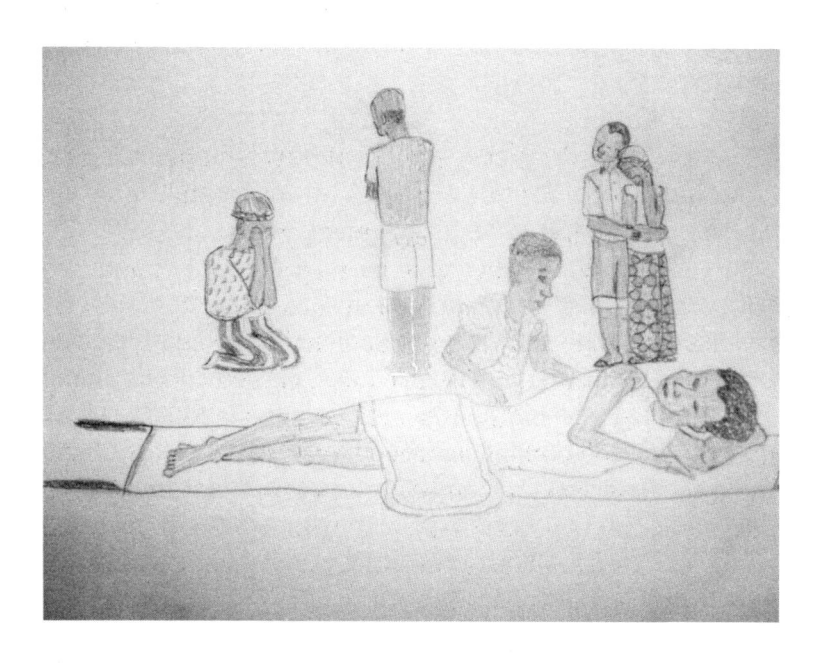

         Every Monday, villagers from Mtindii and nearby villages went to the market. The market was very close to the village. At the market men and women talked about things that happened in their villages during the week between each market day. Anammea liked to go to the market every Monday. She would buy sardines, cassava, cornmeal, salt and many others things she used at home. It was at a place where people brought one week to a close and began a new one. Anammea met a woman called Anabihawa from Kizara village. Bihawa was a friend of Nemphao's. The two women sat at the side of the market where it was relatively quiet. They talked about how their children were doing, especially Bihawa and Nemphao. Anammea shared how her daughter had overheard the women talking about nyungu. She told Anabihawa that after Nemphao heard the news about nyungu, she wanted to know what it was. She had asked so many questions that Anammea was afraid her daughter would not get married. However, she shared that it was good to ask them to obey blindly.

"I worry so much aboutNemphao," She complained. "She talks about things which are not supposed to be talked about by young women her age. She wants to know all about nyungu. You know I cannot tell her because I don't want her to know anything about it. She is someone who can cause problems in the village. She and the other girls of the village have learned to ask about everything. Even the late Anapela complained about how the girls tried to climb an avocado tree. Even the boys seem to be the same way. When Sheshe died, Duku told Kibua and some of the girls that men wanted to receive the women as an inheritance so that they could share the wealth which they had never worked for."

"So the boys seem to agree with the girls?" asked Anabihawa.

"Yes, they do," replied Anammea. "They don't even want to hear anything about the ancestors speaking in Kungu Ja Yamba. I really don't know what to do with the girls and boys of our village. Every man who has a daughter is worried that there are so many Chonges born in the village. They don't listen to anything. They said they would rather see the library burn than keep it going while other people are suffering."

Anammea changed the topic and asked, "So, how is Bihawa doing with her husband and the baby?"

Anabihawa did not reply for a few moments. She started wiping tears from hers eyes. There was silence between the two women for a while. Anammea knew that something was wrong with her friend's daughter. She sat quietly and waited for her to stop crying. She did not want to interfere with her crying. The Washambaa believe that when someone starts to cry, no one should stop them. They don't want the tears to go to another person, so they let the person cry as long as he or she wants. By doing so, the tears stay with the person who was crying.

After about ten minutes, Bihawa's mother stopped crying. She started sharing the story about Bihawa. She told her friend that Bihawa had returned home the week before, and that both she and her husband were very sick. They had gone to the big hospital in the region.

"My daughter is the first one to go," said Bihawa's mother with great sadness. "Her life is over. It is sad that she caught the disease."

"What disease?" asked Anammea.
"She got the disease called AIDS," responded Anabihawa, "No one wants to talk about it. The disease is very dangerous, and there is no treatment for it."
"How did she get that disease?" Anammea asked her friend.

"My daughter's husband went to find a job in the city and he only came home on Tuesdays and Thursdays," Anabihawa explained. "My daughter was not happy about this habit of not coming home every night and when she asked him where he stayed the rest of the nights, he told her

that it was none of her business. He said that she knew he had a full time job and that he had to work hard to make money for the baby who would soon be born. He told Bihara that she knew what her position was in the home and that she was not allowed to question him. According to him, her job was to stay at home and work in the kitchen."
"Did he bring a lot of money for his wife?" Anammea asked.

"No, he didn't," Anabihawa answered. "When he realized that he had gotten that incurable disease, he decided to stay home. Bihawa got very sick, too. She got some money from another friend. With that money, she was able to pay her bus fare and that of her husband. Her husband died two weeks ago."

"That is very sad;" Anammea softly replied. "She might have a baby next week, and they will both die. The baby has also caught the disease. Bihawa's father blames me for allowing her to get married to this boy. He forgot the day he received the bride price and never shared a single shilling with me. I am very sad, Anammea. My daughter is dying."

When she finished the story, Anabihawa started crying again. Many women from Mtindii joined Anammea and Anabihawa. They knew that something was wrong.

The women stood by Anammea and Anabihawa. They did not know what to say to the two women. After a very long silence, Anasesi started the conversation. She talked about the prediction she had from a Busara man that there would be a lot of rain in the village. The rain would allow the people to begin planting maize. The yams and cassava might be spoiled. The rain would begin falling on the twenty-second day following the death of Anapela.

Anasesi asked the women to remind their daughters not to question anything. She said their questions might interfere with the rain. Nengeo asked what was happening between Anammea and the woman said they didn't know. They all wanted to meet Bihawa's mother. As they were talking, Anammea introduced Anabihawa to the women and she told them Anabihawa's daughter was a friend of her own daughter. She explained that Anabihawa was very sad because her daughter had gotten the disease called AIDS. Nengeo suggested that Bihawa be taken to the nuns' hospital, but Anammea explained that there was no treatment for the disease. Anawili was very surprised to find out that the disease couldn't be treated.

Nengeo raised her voice and said, "I heard that Kiao's daughter has the same disease."

"Our daughters are all going to die," responded Anammea. "Nemphao said she wants to be a nun and that she wants to go to school. She always asks so many questions! Maybe she will not die. I told her she would not find out what nyungu is. She does not want to get married. I am worried but, well, I guess she will be happy in that way."

"They will call her Chonge," warned Anabihawa.

"She is already Chonge," chimed in Anasesi. "That girl scares me. Sometimes she even tries to climb trees!"

"Wait until I tell her about her friend Bihawa," Anammea sadly remarked.

"She will surely never get married after hearing that!" Nengeo joined in, "Do you remember that when my husband died, the men wanted me to be given as an inheritance? I refused, and I decided to pick my own son Kibua."

Anasesi nodded and said, "They did not like it when you picked Kibua. They always call you a grown-up Chonge."

"But when Anapela died, no one was given to Sapela as an inheritance," Anammea reminded them. "Why should be it be a problem for Nengeo?"

"Look, our daughters are dying because of men," Nengeo spoke out with a strong voice. "Bihawa is going to die. She will never see her child grow up because of a man."

"Her child, too, will never grow up because the baby also got the disease," Anabihawa added.

"So is the baby going to die?" asked Anammea.

"Yes," replied Nengeo. "I heard that the disease kills the mother, the father, and the baby."

"Her husband died two weeks ago," Anabihawa said solemnly. "She and the baby will be the next ones to die."

Anammea felt compelled to speak out strongly, "Look, the Busara need to talk about this disease. They are keeping quiet, and they are keeping our daughters from going to school. We need to help our daughters so they can stop crying. Let us look toward Kungu Ja Yamba. If it gives water and life to our villages, it should also give life to our children. We have cried and there is no one to wipe away our tears. Who is going to help us out when our daughters are dying? They don't go to school and they can't speak out about anything. It will look like we want to keep Chonge in our village if we let our daughters speak out, but the time has come for us to make some changes. This should be the day to call upon the spirits of our mothers."

When Anammea had spoken for a long time, Anasesi started spitting on the ground and said, "When this market day ends, may a lot of girls become pregnant to bear daughters who can not be Chonges. When they are born, they are born to be mothers. May our daughters grow up to be what they want to be. Motherhood should be their first choice. May my daughter Nemphao grow up to wipe away the tears of all women!"

As soon as Anammea finished speaking, Anabihawa solemnly declared, "May the day my daughter dies be the beginning of a new day in which the Busara men will no longer have the power to control our children's lives."

"When our daughters speak, may our sons listen," Nengeo earnestly declared.

The women all bent their heads toward the center of the group. None of them said anything more. One by one, they silently disappeared. Each one went to her own home to share with her daughters the story about Bihawa's sickness. By the time the market had closed, almost every house in the village had learned about that sickness. Nemphao and many other young girls cried hard for a very long time. Bihawa died two weeks after the women talked about her in the market. With great sadness, Nemphao and the other girls and boys attended Bihawa's funeral.

Biography

Sister Evetha Kilamba is a member of the Congregation of Our Lady of Usambara (COLU) in Tanzania, East Africa. She was born in the 1960s in the Tanga region, Lushoto district, in a Village called Gare at a particular place called Mtindii. Sister Kilamba is one of 14 children. Unlike all her sisters, Kilamba chose a different life rather than getting married. In 1983, she joined the COLU sisters where she became a nun in December of 1986.

From 1989 to 1992, Sister Kilamba attended her Ordinary Level education at St. Mary's Secondary School. She then studied the Advanced Level at Dakawa High School from 1993 to 1995. After she graduated from Dakawa High School, she attended Mpwapwa Teacher Training College from 1996 to 1998 and she acquired a diploma in teaching. In 2000, Dr. Robert Miller of Nazareth College of Rochester offered Sister Kilamba a scholarship to Nazareth College of Rochester in Rochester, NY, USA. Sister Kilamba majored in English and minored in Women's Studies. She graduated in the spring of 2004 and began a master's degree in education. Sister Kilamba wrote this story while she was a graduate student at Nazareth College.

Soon after finishing graduate school, Sister Kilamba is planning to return to Tanzania. Her goal is to encourage education for women and the whole society. She believes that educating a woman is educating the whole society. She will thus encourage girls to never give up their education. *Voices of Change* is one of the ways through which Sister Kilamba encourages women and people around the world to make education a top priority. She says, "Education should never make us forget our culture, but we should not let our culture cripple us. Let us cry out for so that changes will be made. I hope you hear the voices in this story. May they inspire you to begin making changes right now."